D0685890

CHINESE BONSAI
The Art of Penjing

Ilona Lesniewicz
and Li Zhimin

BLANDFORD PRESS
LONDON · NEW YORK · SYDNEY

First published in the UK 1988
by Blandford Press
an imprint of Cassell plc
Artillery House,
Artillery Row,
London SW1P 1RT

English language edition copyright © 1988 Blandford Publishing Ltd.

Originally published in German as
Penjing: Miniaturbäume aus China
by Ilona Lesniewicz and Li Zhimin
World copyright © 1987 Verlag Bonsai Centrum,
Heidelberg.

Distributed in the United States by
Sterling Publishing Co, Inc,
2 Park Avenue, New York, NY 10016

Distributed in Australia by
Capricorn Link (Australia) Pty Ltd
PO Box 665, Lane Cove, NSW 2066

British Library Cataloguing in Publication Data

Lesniewicz, Ilona
    Chinese bonsai : the art of penjing.
    1. Bonsai
    I. Title   II. Zhimin, Li   III. Penjing -
    miniature baume aus china. *English*
    635.9'772   SB433.5

ISBN 0 7137 2013 1

All rights reserved.
No part of this book may be reproduced
or transmitted in any form or by any means, electronic
or mechanical, including photocopying, recording
or any information storage and retrieval system,
without permission in writing
from the Publisher.

Translation from the German by Astrid Mick
Photography by Achim Bunz
Typeset by August Typesetting, St. Helens, Lancs.
Printed in Portugal by Printer Portuguesa

Contents

Acknowledgements

Our thanks go to all those who
contributed
towards the creation of this book:

Mrs Xie Yongping;
Mr Gan Weilin, Beijing;
Mr Wu Yu-Cheng, Guangzhou;
Mr Bi Shu Chang, Wuhan;
Mr Wu Zong Jun, Nanjing;
Mr Liu Gouzhao, Mr Hu Liangming
and Mr Zhang Goubao, Wuxi; Mr Bai Chuanru;
Mr Zhu Yongyuan, Suzhou;
Mr Zhong Boxi, Mayor;
Mr Sze Tien Tung and
Mrs Feng Xiang Zhen, Hangzhou;
Mr Wan Rui Ming, Yangzhou;
Mr Zhang Zhiguang; Mr Lu Dinggou;
Mr Wang Zemin;
Mr Zhang Llan Duan, Shanghai;
Mrs Ma Hui Fen, Frankfurt;
Mrs Wong, Paris;
and all the employees of the
Landscape and Architecture Company of China.
To Dr Gerhard Andres, Munich,
for the photo of the tomb painting.

Foreword

In China, miniature trees and miniature landscapes are called 'penjing'. We know from picture rolls of the Song dynasty (AD 960–1279) that exhibitions of these precious trees were already taking place in China hundreds of years ago.

We are delighted, almost 1000 years later, to be able to show you some interesting and valuable penjing from many different regions of China. Some of these works of art were given to us on loan and will be returned to China, others remain in Germany and are on view at the Bonsai Museum in Heidelberg.

The inspiration for our exhibition came from Dr Wolfgang R. Habbell, and without his support, this project could not have been realised. Consequently, Wolfgang Hundbiss, Achim Bunz and I were able to travel to China in the autumn of 1986 to visit the sources of this ancient and fascinating art form.

We were helped in our efforts to find 'the right places' by our colleagues of many years' standing in the world of professional gardening – and by Marianne Beuchert's friendly connections with the LAC (The Landscape and Architecture Company of China).

Achim Bunz captured this journey visually in his photographs. The informative text of this book was compiled by Li Zhimin and Ilona Lesniewicz.

My grateful thanks go to all the aforementioned people. We hope that our efforts will win many new friends for this most beautiful art form.

Paul Lesniewicz, Heidelberg

The History of Penjing

While the peoples of Europe were just beginning to clear dark forests and cultivate meagre grasslands, the art of gardening was flourishing at a high level in China.

In that country, which nature has endowed with a multitude of plant forms and an immense wealth of shapes, garden architects were already beginning, on the Emperor's orders, to build artificial lake and island landscapes, or to copy the bizarre rocky formation of the Chinese mountains in the Palace gardens. In this way, the surrounding impressive landscape of China was set out in miniature. According to an old legend from those times, the magician Jiang-feng possessed the power of reducing these landscapes even further. He could recreate them with rocks, mountains, trees, rivers, houses, people and animals – on a tray!

Maybe the beginnings of penjing art go back to that early period of Chinese history, for the culture of pot-plants was also already known. Representations of flowers and shrubs in pots, the so-called *penzai*, on wall paintings in tombs of the Han period (206 BC–AD 220) are proof of this.

The Chinese word *penzai* is pronounced *bonsai* in Japanese. Buddhist monks from China brought the 'living sculptures' to Japan in the tenth and eleventh centuries, and the Japanese were the first to introduce the miniature trees to an amazed public at the Paris Global Exhibition in 1878. In China, single trees and landscapes in bowls were probably called penjing from the end of the Ming dynasty (1368–1644).

The oldest known representation of a miniature landscape was found among the wall paintings in the burial chamb-ers of Prince Zhang Huai of the Tang dynasty (AD 618–907). These paintings convey a lively impression of everyday life at the court.

In that period, which was so appreciative of art, the beauty of nature was celebrated by poets and painters alike, and glorified in their works. Chinese landscape painting influenced both the fashioning of gardens and the gardening works of art – penjing. These penjing became the much admired, indeed revered focal points in the gardens of the Imperial Palace, and in the following centuries their creation became a favourite pastime of artists and the educated nobility.

In the Song dynasty (960–1279), the art of penjing reached a high level. An early example of penjing techniques, still in use today, can be studied in the famous 'pictorial rolls of the eighteen sages' from this period, at the Imperial Palace in Peking. The two pine penjing depicted in these rolls hardly resemble the graceful young treelets of the wall paintings in the tomb of Crown Prince Zhang Huai, but are, rather, gnarled tree veterans with thick trunks and vigorous new shoots. These pines were formed from tree roots, in order to produce miniature trees which look old. In addition to tree-root penjing and the traditional landscapes made of plants, stones and water, people now began to set only bizarrely formed stones or rocks in bowls of water, thereby creating stone-water penjing. In a book from this period, called *Yunlin Shipu*, over 116 types of stone are listed for the creation of penjing. In the following Yuan dynasty (1279–1368) there was great enthusiasm for miniature penjing. A poet of this period, Ding He-nian, wrote poems about the *Xie-Zi-Penjing* of

Wall painting in
the tomb of Prince Zhang Huai
of the Tang dynasty.

6

the monk Yun Shang-ren of Pingjiang (*Xie-Zi* means small or tiny), and he mentioned that *Xie-Zi-Penjing* were very much influenced by the rock-water-landscape paintings of Yun Shangren's time. Further, Yun Shang-ren's penjing were extraordinary in that one could 'observe the large within the small all at once'. This concept became an important principle for the creation of penjing in the following centuries, and has remained so to this day.

In the Ming dynasty many books were written on penjing. As landscape painting always held an important place in Chinese art, penjing artists found models for their works of art in the extremely poetical and highly idealized depictions of famous Chinese landscapes. In order to copy them faithfully in miniature, natural stones from the regions being represented were worked, sawn up, and glued together, and then assembled in perspective to create a landscape tableau. In this way 'three-dimensional paintings' ensued, 'silent poems' admired by all, or 'living sculptures'. The bizarre, impressive pines of the Tian Mu Mountain were a well-known, favourite subject of this period.

An ancient juniper penjing from the end of the Ming dynasty from the Buddhist temple of Tian Ning can still be seen today in Yangzhou. It is two chi (approximately 65 cm) high, its trunk as crooked 'as a bearded dragon'. Only a third of the bark of the tree remains. The old dragon lifts his head and carries a 'cloud layer' which was formed out of the horizontal branches, and is slightly rounded off towards the crown. This tree had the correct size for its period, and from then on miniature trees which could be placed on a small tea table were considered to be especially valuable. Penjing which, because of their size, had to be set up in the garden or in a pavilion, were not as valuable.

In the Qing dynasty (1644–1911) these now generally well-known and highly prized miniature trees and miniature landscapes were the focal points in the gardens of refined and wealthy families. Often, a penjing gardener was taken into service for the care of these valuable objects. In Suzhou, one of the major metropolitan art centres in that giant country, there was an annual competition for the most beautiful penjing. It was considered an honour to participate in the competition, and those families who did so carefully kept the secrets of the gardening art of their penjing masters from each other.

The penjing masters were excellent craftsmen. Traditionally, they allowed themselves to be inspired in their creations by the painting, poetry and calligraphy of their time and region. In this way were developed the major

Detail from a painting of
the Qing dynasty (1644–1911).

7

penjing styles, in the larger cities which were the centres of all artistic creativity, and the various styles are now named after them.

The theory for the still new penjing style in Guangzhou (Canton), the so-called Lingnan style (the idea of the tree in this case is rather realistic, following the way it is in nature), was founded by the Lingnan school of painting at the end of the last century. Earlier on, penjing styles had had very poetic names. From the Ming and Qing periods have been handed down to us the 'pagoda style' of Yangzhou, the 'style of the dancing dragon' of Anhui, the 'earthworm style' of Sichuan, and others. Today, different standards are held within the art of penjing. The trees look more natural, are no longer so bizarrely formed – over-laden with artistic ideas – because the popular Lingnan school has done some spring-cleaning among the ideas of the other penjing schools, but the basic themes of ancient times can still be recognised clearly in the modern Suzhou, Yangzhou, Sichuan and Anhui styles.

In modern China, after 1949, one of the leading 'ten generals' formulated the goal for artistic endeavour in the newly founded People's Republic of China quite in the tradition of his country: 'Great works of art glorify nature!' So penjing culture continues to be cherished and developed further as people's art. During the upheavals of the Cultural Revolution, many irreplaceable trees were lost forever. Today, the Chinese are trying to awaken interest in these miniatures especially among the young. China is an immense country with some regions extending widely into several climatic zones. Influenced by geographical factors, each landscape has its own manifold varieties of plants and forms, and therefore an almost infinite number of motifs for penjing art. The different techniques also extend possibilities for forming and shaping. Also, there are naturally great differences in the way each artist mirrors himself in his work, in his ideas, and in his ideals of nature expressed in this art.

The Wan Rui Ming
family in Yangzhou: well-known penjing
masters for many generations.

Styles of Penjing

The Lingnan School

'Cut the trunk and let the branches grow' – this is the principle according to which penjing are formed following the Lingnan method in Guangzhou (Canton).

Apricots, camellias, sagaretias, carmonas, elms and orange jasmine are the preferred plants for use, as they rapidly produce new shoots. After the first cut (the trunk and the branches are shortened), the little tree is allowed to grow until the branches and the shoots have reached the correct thickness, and then it is cut back again. Each cutting back causes a further forking of the branches. Using this method, harmonious proportions are attained between trunk, branches and leaves. The artists are proud of the fact that their trees are formed properly, right through to the tiniest branchlet. The miniature trees of the Lingnan school are equivalent in their appearance to their relatives in nature. They are 'created by human endeavour, but are free of artistic ideas and ideals regarding shape'. Penjing of this style are especially popular in the West, and are also becoming more popular in China.

The Shanghai (Hai) School

Very similar to the Lingnan style, the modern Hai style has elevated the principle of 'forming according to the appearance of the tree in nature'. In this case, the miniature trees are formed not only by cutting and then letting them grow, but also by the use of other techniques such as tying and wiring. However, the artist's efforts are to remain as invisible as possible. They use mainly serissa, stone yew, juniper, box, pseudolarix and pines for the creation of their penjing.

The Suzhou (Su) School

A typical example of a miniature tree in the Su style is an old, gnarled, thick trunk with delicate branches full of green leaves. This attractive contrast of old and young makes the tree come alive. 'A withered tree experiences another spring,' say the Chinese. Many penjing of this style are created from old tree roots. Preferred are such deciduous species as elms, apricots, maples and pomegranate trees.

In another direction of the Su school, the penjing have a more regular shape. The

Sagaretia penjing
of the Suzhou School.

9

trunk grows straight up or is only slightly inclined; all the branches of the left side of the tree and those of the right side grow out parallel, one above the other. Each of these profusely forking branches is cut into a round half-cushion shape. A trunk with six of these round discs is called a 'six platform'. The three discs stretching to the back are called 'the three carriers'. A single disc forms the apex of the tree. Viewed from above, such a penjing looks like a large flower with nine petals.

The Yangzhou (Yang) School

You would not find a single straight branch in the 'cloud style' trees of the Yang school. A tree formed in the Yang style has a twisted trunk and extremely contorted main branches (at least three twists every one chi, which equals $\frac{1}{3}$ m), which in turn fork again

A pine penjing with 'cloud discs' and an almost straight multi-trunk.

in an equally contorted fashion to form the smaller branches. The separate main branches form thick storeys, regular 'cloud discs'. Seen from below, each main branch looks like the woven seat of a stool. At the crown of the tree the flat 'cloud discs' are a circular shape, and in the middle and lower parts more oval, rather like the palm of a hand. Their number is dependent on the size and shape of the penjing. They can have anything from one to nine discs. The trunk and branches are formed into this artistic shape by clever use of binding with palm fibres. In this Yang style there is a preference for the use of box, gingko and elm.

The Sichuan (Chuan) School

Development of the Chuan style in Sichuan province is based on the rich multitude of shapes in the province's landscape, and on its highly developed gardening culture. In contrast to the Lingnan method, it is a very artistic style.

The trunk of the young tree and its main branches are tied up tightly with palm-fibre twine right from the start, so that the tree experiences gradual reshaping according to a set pattern. With all trees of the Chuan style the trunk is twisted upwards, snake-like, or even in steps. The trunk twists sinuously like a dragon about an (imaginary) pillar. Very often, the number of twists and also the number of branches are set. For example, with one type of tree the trunk grows in five curves upwards, and has 10 main branches which lead off in alternating pairs. All the branches pointing in the same direction are either almost horizontal, or just slightly inclined.

With another shape in the Chuan style, the main characteristic is the visible and extremely entwined rootwork which passes up into a regularly twisted trunk.

The Chuan school prefers apricot trees, ornamental apple trees, serissa and gingkos for penjing.

Shapes in Penjing

Tree Shapes

Miniature trees can be classified not only by the school or style, but also by the direction of growth of the trunk and branches. There is a standing shape (the trunk grows straight up), a crooked-trunk shape, (the trunk is twisted snake-like upwards), a lying shape (the trunk actually lies across the bowl), an 'over-hanging cliff' shape (the trunk and branches are curved downwards over the edge of the bowl, which is usually high), a root shape, and a jungle shape. The growing and tending of the penjing are carried out according to the characteristics of the plant chosen.

Many Chinese miniature trees have their own, extremely poetic name, or have been associated with a poem. So they are called by names such as 'sculpture of green jade', 'green bells ringing in the morning', 'an apple tree puts on its red dress', 'standing in a cold autumn', 'an old lady makes herself beautiful', and 'a tiger is resting'.

Miniature Landscapes

The word 'penjing' is used in China both for single trees and also for miniature landscapes. In Guilin, Guangxi province, stone and water penjing are often formed using local stones, and themes are chosen based on mountain and water landscapes of the Li river valley, whose bizarre rocky mountains, rising needle-like, are famous worldwide. Other penjing are copies of the high mountain ranges of the north, or of the island landscapes of the south. 'Even when as small as a child's foot, it appears ten thousand Li far, and in the tiniest place we see thousands of mountains,' (1 Li = 500 m).

There are three types of miniature landscape:

1 the stone and water penjing. Only stones placed in bowls of water are used for this;
2 earth and stone penjing (without water). Earth and stones form a mountain landscape. Water can be represented symbolically by white gravel;
3 the plant, earth, stone and water penjing.

For the forming of these 'three-dimensional paintings' the following rules of perspective apply: for the distance, lighter colours, smaller plants and stones, less detail, perhaps moss instead of trees, flatter stones for long mountain ranges, and their summits not so clearly sculpted as are stones for the foreground. In the latter, darker colours are used, larger shapes, and more detail.

'Seeing the large within the small'; the mountain landscape of Huangshan – copied in miniature.

Someone's inner world outside: penjing on a windowsill.

14 Penjing: a piece of poetry in everyday Chinese life.

The geometrical shapes used in the art of forming both trees and
ornaments have been handed down for centuries in China.

Searched for by the master, and found: a tree before
its transformation into a work of art.

A marble slab, stones, earth, plants: every day anew 'the creation of the earth'.

The branches of a yew are gently shaped with palm fibres.

22

Evening in the famous Wan Jing Shan Zhuang Garden of
Suzhou. In the foreground is an ancient juniper, planted in an
antique bowl. The bowl, shaped like a lotus flower, came from
the well-known potteries of Ishing.

Decorative gateways present a special first glimpse, and invite one to enter beautifully tended penjing gardens.

In the tradition of the ancestors: cultivating plants in large pottery bowls.

In a Chinese nursery the most important task first thing in the morning is watering.

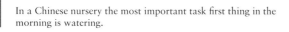

The art of Chinese pottery-making is rich in shapes and colours. Here, a precious old bowl from the nineteenth century with beautiful flower and animal ornamentation.

Bowls stacked in the corner of a penjing nursery. Their colours and shapes indicate the nursery's proximity to the Guangzhou region.

Money is counted, there are last thoughts about other important purchases – but the love of penjing wins out!

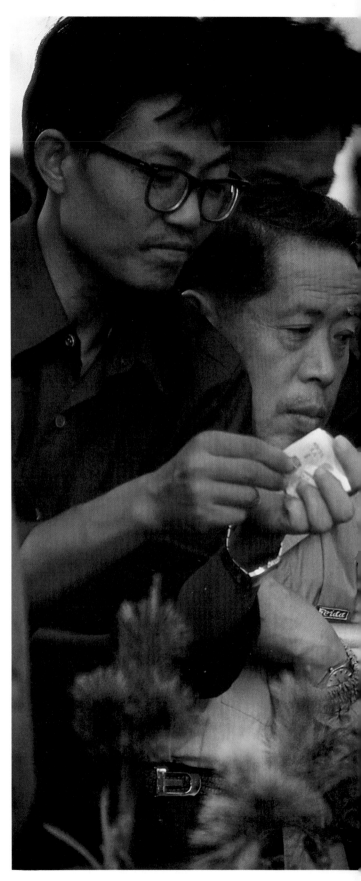

A small nursery proudly presents its most beautiful trees in an exhibition.

Elm, height: 70 cm, Suzhou.
Dug up in the mountains, and allowed to remain in its natural
shape, this tree has been planted in a bowl, the decoration of
which reminds one of the tree's original home.

Sagaretia, height: 70 cm, Suzhou.
A harmoniously shaped tree with a lively, flecked bark pattern
on the lower part of the trunk.

Sagaretia, height: 120 cm, Hangzhou.
For Buddhist monks in early China, the miniature trees were
'Verdant steps leading to heaven'.

Gingko, height: 65 cm, Yangzhou.
Gingko trees are among the most ancient trees in the world, and
have always belonged to the history of humankind in East Asia.
This Gingko penjing was formed in the traditional Yang style: a
gently twisted trunk with horizontal branch-steps in the lower
half, and a circular crown.

Box, height: 50 cm, Yangzhou.
This tree is an example of the highly creative penjing artform of
the Yang school. Using palm fibres, the trunk and branches have
been twisted in a snake-like design, and the branches then
shaped into 'cloud discs'.

Sagaretia, height: 40 cm, Nanjing.
'Rearing horse in front of the two pagodas'. The trunk of this
ancient penjing is almost completely dead, except for the narrow
layers of bark. These supply the branches with water and
nutrients, and keep the tree alive.

Carmona, height: 110 cm, Guangzhou.
A tree from the 'drunken temple garden' in Guangzhou. It is
growing in a green-glazed, octagonal, Cantonese dish, which in
turn is placed on a highly decorative, multi-coloured, glazed
pillar.

Sagaretia, height: 30 cm, Nanjing.
Unusual shapes for both tree and container, delicately matched
together. The tree's roots protrude horizontally over the edge of
the bowl, and then move upward into the almost vertical trunk.
The branches on the left side form a harmonious
counterbalance.

Elm, height: 90 cm, Suzhou, Zhuo Zheng Garden.
This tree looks as it does in nature. Elm penjing are robust,
unfussy trees with thick trunks and small leaves.

Three-pointed maple, height: 80 cm, Suzhou.
This example of a maple penjing has several trunks growing out
of one root. The branches together form a scalene triangle.

Elm, height: 130 cm, Wuhan, Jie Fang Park.
It is often difficult to determine which is the front of a penjing,
namely the side which shows up best the structure of the tree.
The observer will have to decide which aspect of this old tree
reveals most of its secret.

Yew, height: 120 cm, Hangzhou.
The perfect replica of a tree in nature. The plant container of
white marble emphasises the aura of this majestic tree.

Pine (*Pinus parviflora glauca*), height: 130 cm,
Hangzhou, Zhui Jing Gardens.
Two trees which have grown into a single living unit.

Pine (*Pinus parviflora glauca*), height: 70 cm, Suzhou.
Penjing such as this can sometimes be found in Suzhou. A tree
which was formed freely and not in the typical Suzhou style.

Pine (*Pinus nigra*), height: 75 cm, Suzhou.
Hand-finished marble dishes heighten the effect of these two
miniature trees. Just like the *Pinus parviflora*, the
Pinus nigra wishes to do no more than remind one of its big
brothers in nature.

Yew, height: 78 cm, Suzhou.
From a very small pot rises a tree radiating peace. It has
beautifully shaped branches.

Elm, height: 75 cm, Wuhan, East Lake Garden.
The ends of the profusely branching main stems of this elm have
been cut into thick, round half-cushions, and appear as a single
continuous crown. The branches are supported by a strongly
contorted trunk.

Elm, height: 80 cm, Suzhou, Wan Jing Shan Zhuang Garden.
An impression of the mountains: surrounding a fissured rock,
two elms have been planted of varying thickness and height.

Elm, height: 90 cm, Suzhou.
This penjing is also to be seen in the Wan Jing Shan Zhuang
Garden. Bizarre shapes of tree and stone complement each
other perfectly.

Sagaretia, height: 50 cm, Nanjing.
Many penjing have names or poems associated with them.
This tree resembles in its shape the Chinese glyph for
'double happiness'.

Sagaretia, height: 40 cm, Nanjing.
The gnarled, old trunk reminds one of a fabulous beast resting
in the shade of the branches, which have been shaped into
circular half-cushions.

Yew, height: 15 cm, Shanghai.
This tree, in a cascade shape, belongs to the type of miniature
penjing which are becoming more and more popular. This size
(15–25 cm high) is preferred for shaping yews, *Pinus parviflora*,
sagaretia, serissa and juniper.

Sagaretia, height: 30 cm, Nanjing.
A small, graceful treelet, formed from an older piece of root.
The brick-red colour of the clay pot contrasts well with the fresh
green colour of the leaves.

Sagaretia, height: 80 cm, Wuxi.
What is created by nature, and what by human design? In the
case of this bizarre tree-root penjing, dug up in the mountains,
only the branches have been cut again and again into
round half-cushions.

Elm, height: 120 cm, Wuxi.
This old elm-foundling is from the same collection, but at a
'younger' stage of shaping. Its branches are still in the process of
being shaped into circular storeys.

Memories of Chinese landscapes.

Appendix: Useful Addresses

Federation of British Bonsai Societies

Secretary, Rivendale, 14 Somerville Road,
  Sutton Coldfield, West Midlands B73 6JA.
Bedfordshire B.S., 21 Bibshall Crescent,
  Dunstable, Beds.
Bonsai Kai of London, 39 West Square,
  London SE11 4SP.
Bristol B.S., 35 Clevedon Road, Failand, Bristol,
  Avon BS8 3UL.
British B.A., Flat D, 15 St John's Park, Blackheath,
  London SE3 7TH.
Cotswold B.S., The Gardens, Catley, Nr Bosbury,
  Herefordshire HR8 1QF.
Croydon B.C., Tanglewood, Coldharbour,
  Common Road, Lingfield, Surrey RH7 6BZ.
East Midlands Bonsai, Greenwood Gardens,
  Ollerton Road, Arnold, Notts NG5 8PR.
Humberside B.S., 43 The Dales, Cottingham,
  North Humberside HU16 5JS.
Humnanby B.C., 34 Hungate Lane, Humnanby,
  Yorkshire YO14 ONP.
Kew Kai Bonsai, 7 Crane Park Road, Whitton,
  Middx TW2 6DF.
Lincoln B.S., 5 Home Close, Bracebridge Heath,
  Lincoln LN4 2LP.
Manchester B.S., 160 Cheadle Old Road, Edgeley,
  Stockport, Cheshire.
Middlesex B.S., 48 Tregenna Avenue, South Harrow,
  Middx HA2 8QS
Midland B.S., 46 Hodge Hill Common,
  Birmingham BS36 8AG.
Milton Keynes B.S., 20 Station Terrace,
  Great Linford, Milton Keynes MK14 5AP.
National B.S., 4 Meadow Brow, Banks Road,
  Southport PR9 8JG.
Norfolk B.A., 7 Broadland Close, Worlingham,
  Beccles, Suffolk NR34 7AT.
Northern Ireland B.S., 6 Marina Park, Belfast BT5 6BA.

Scottish B.A., 2 Humbie Holdings, Kirknewton,
  Midlothian, Scotland, EH27 8DS.
Solent B.S., 32 Kingston Road, Gosport,
  Hants, PO12 3LL.
Southend B.S., 45 Brunswick Road, Southend-on-Sea,
  Essex SS1 2UH.
Sussex B.S., 13 Southway, Burgess Hill,
  West Sussex RH15 9SS.
Waltham Forest, 66 Selwyn Avenue, Highams Park,
  London E4 9LR.
Yorkshire B.A., 38 Green Lane, Cookridge, Leeds,
  W. Yorks LS16 7LP.

Send an S.A.E. with all correspondence.

Main UK Bonsai Dealers

Bourne Bridge Nurseries, Oak Hill Road,
  Stapleford Abbotts, Romford, Essex.
Bromage and Young, St Mary's Gardens, Worplesdon,
  Surrey GU3 3RS.
Glenbrook Nursery, Stone Edge Batch, Twickenham,
  Clevedon BS21 6SE.
Greenwood Gardens, Ollerton Road, Arnold, Notts.
Herons Bonsai Nursery, Dawn & Peter Chan, Wire Mill
  Lane, New Chapel, Nr. Lingfield, Surrey RH7 6HJ.
Middle Earth Bonsai, 249 Lytham Road, Southport,
  Merseyside.
Meads End Bonsai, Forewood Lane, Crowhurst, Battle,
  Sussex TN33 9AB.
Tokonoma Bonsai, 14 London Road, Shenley, Radlett,
  Herts.
Potters Garden Bonsai, The Boat House, Potters Lane,
  Samlesbury, Preston.
Price and Adams, Cherry Trees, 22 Burnt Hill Road,
  Wrecclesham, Surrey.
Adreanne Weller, St Mary's Garden, Worplesdon,
  Surrey.

International Contacts

Australia
Mr Lindsay Bebb, 8 Fegen Drive,
  Moorooka, QLD, 4105 Australia
J. Farman, Victoria Bonsai
  Association, 14 Sussex Street,
  Brighton 3186, Victoria, Australia
Mr Frank Hocking, Bonsai in
  Australia, 14 Newhall Avenue,
  Moonie Ponds, 3039 Australia
Mr Jim Scott, National Bonsai
  Association, c/o 22 Burraga
  Avenue, Terrey Hills, N.S.W. 2084,
  Australia

Austria
Osterreichischer B C,
  Zaunmullerstrasse 1, A–4020 Linz,
  Austria

Belgium
BBF–FBB Fazantenlaan 31, 1900
  Overijse, Belgium

Denmark
Dansk B Selskab, Sobredden 22 2820,
  Gentofte, Denmark

E. Germany
Heidrun Hunger, Cothnerstr 9, 7022
  Leipzig

European Bonsai Association
G.M. De Beule, European Bonsai
  Association, Heliotropenlaan 3,
  1030 Brussel, Belgium

France
French Bonsai Federation, FFB, Allee
  de Duras, St Benait la Foret, 37500
  Chinon, France
Club Parisienne Du Bonsai, 29 Rue
  Du Roi De Sicilie, 75004 Paris,
  France

Finland
Matti Makinen, Kukkakauppojen
  Tukky Oy, Valuraudantie 17, SF–
  00700, Helsinki

Greece
Nicolas Rountis, Roynth, Kifissiasn
  Ave 105A, (Erychros Stavros),
  Athens

Hungary
Tamas Biro, Dipl. Ing. of Hort., 1126
  Budapest, Margarata Str. 17

India
Indian Bonsai Society, Mrs L. Jhaveri,
  105 Samundra Mahal, Dr Annie
  Besant Road, Worli, Bombay, India

Ireland
Irish Bonsai Society, 18 Strand Road,
  Merrion, Dublin 4

Italy
Bonsai Clubs D'Italia, Str. Mongreno,
  341 10132 Torino, Italy
G. Bruno, Assoc. Italiana Bonsai,
  2 50136 Firenze, Italy

Japan
Mr Y. Nagase, Kawaguchi Bonsai
  Association, 2–1–1 Aoki,
  Kawaguchi City, Saitama-Pref.
  Japan
Nippon Bonsai Association, 3–42
  Ueno-Koen, Daito-ku, Tokyo,
  Japan

Index